Palette knife

X-Acto knife

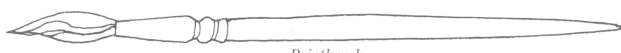

Paintbrush

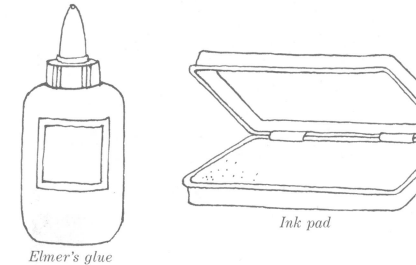

Elmer's glue

Ink pad

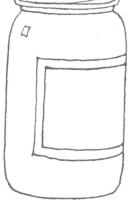

Tempera paint

PRINTMAKING

by
Harlow Rockwell

DOUBLEDAY & COMPANY, INC., GARDEN CITY, NEW YORK

ISBN: 0-385-01813-4 Trade

0-385-01816-9 Prebound

Library of Congress Catalog Card Number 73-78479

Copyright © 1973 by Harlow Rockwell

All Rights Reserved

Printed in the United States of America

9   8   7   6   5   4   3   2

CONTENTS

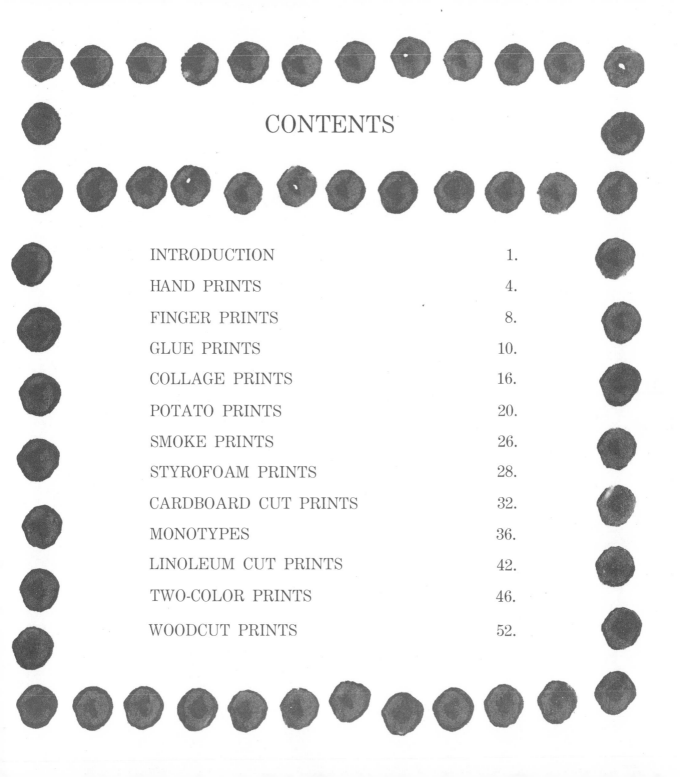

Potato print

By Olly — age 6

INTRODUCTION

Printmaking is the process of transferring an image from one surface to another, either as a single or multiple edition. Whatever surface you use to print from, it is fun to make a print. You will see in this book that it is easy as well. You need not have any previous knowledge of printmaking. The materials are readily available and inexpensive. The processes described are simple and safe and require little adult supervision. When it comes to the use of knives and gouges, some supervision is advisable, but most techniques need no sharp cutting tools.

The book could be useful to parents, teachers, scout leaders, Sunday school teachers, camp counselors, and others, introducing this art form to young beginners. It progresses from the simplest methods to those which are somewhat more difficult. Even techniques which are basically simple can produce interesting and beautiful results when done with imagination and style.

1

An interesting feature of printmaking is that the print seems to take on some of the character of the material printed from. Wood offers its own definite quality or texture, linoleum also, and so on. As a result a print can be influenced in subtle and pleasing ways that were not necessarily planned. And of course you can reproduce a drawing once or many times. Children can design and print posters for school events, make prints to give away to friends, print holiday cards for their own use or to sell to others, make colorful wrapping paper and many other things.

The stationery store can supply some materials, such as Elmer's glue, ink pad, Scotch tape, carbon paper, pencils, tracing paper, newsprint paper, and poster board. From an art supply store you can obtain linoleum, rice paper, tempera paint, water-base block-printing ink, X-Acto knife, small paintbrush, linoleum gouge, wood gouge, and brayer. Usually a lumberyard has scraps or ends of boards for sale, which can be used for woodcuts. Many useful things are found around the house, such as pieces of Styrofoam, cardboard, corrugated board, kitchen knife, cookie sheet, pie tin, miscellaneous objects for collage prints, and so on.

Make some prints and experience a similar satisfaction to that of some of our greatest artists.

Cardboard cut print

HAND PRINTS

1. Take a plate or paper plate and a jar of tempera paint. After stirring thoroughly, pour some paint onto the plate.

2. Place your hand on the paint.

3. Then press your hand onto a piece of white or colored paper.

4. When you lift your hand you have made a print.

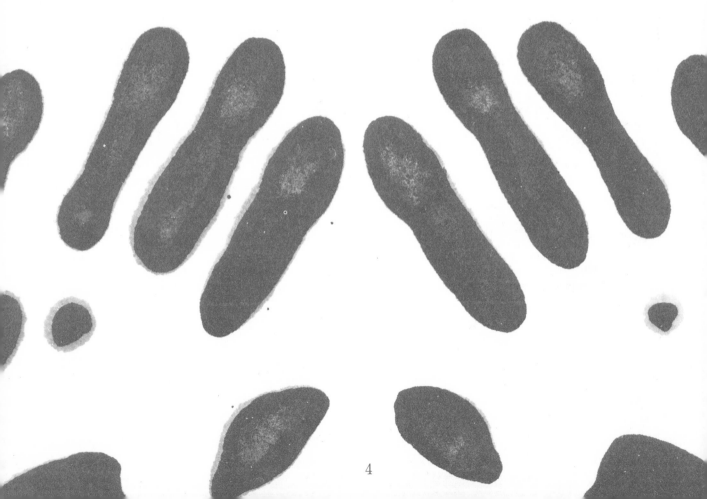

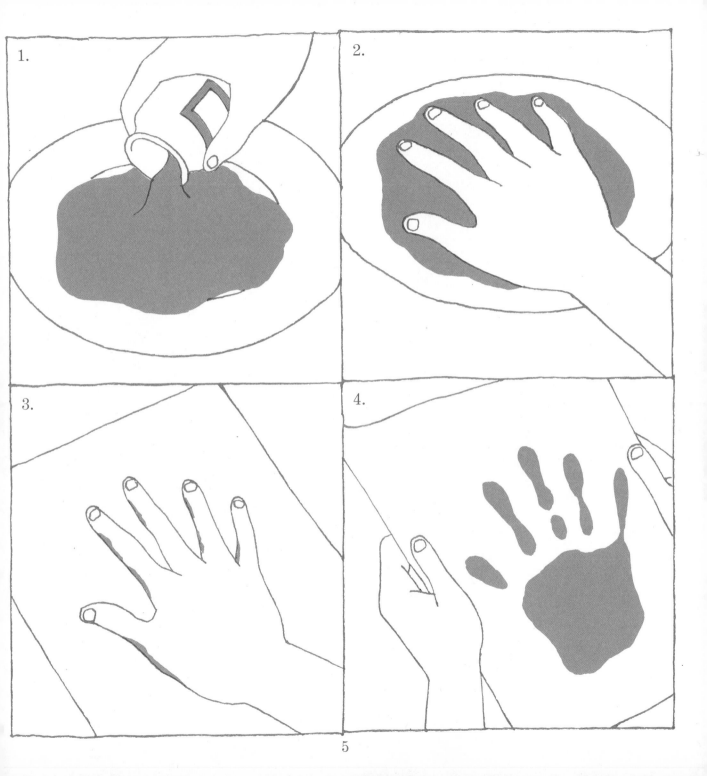

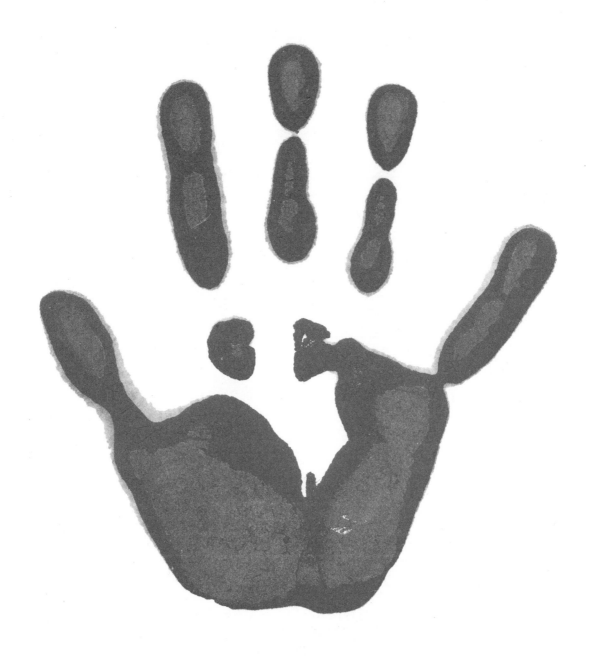

Hand print   *By Lizzy—age 11*

6

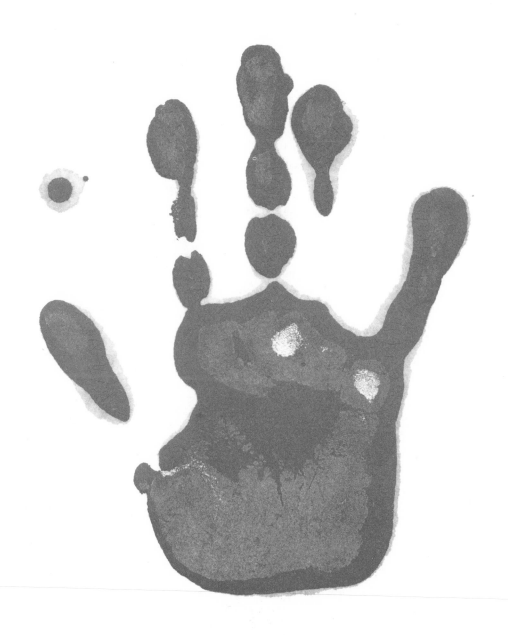

By Olly—age 6

FINGER PRINTS

Finger prints can be made with an ink pad (for rubber stamps).

1. Place the ball of your finger or thumb on an open ink pad.

2. Then press your finger carefully onto a piece of paper. Lift it.

3. There is your finger print showing the individual whorls which are yours alone.

4. Make many finger prints. Add to them by drawing hats, feet, ears, etc.

By Lizzy—age 11

By Olly—age 6

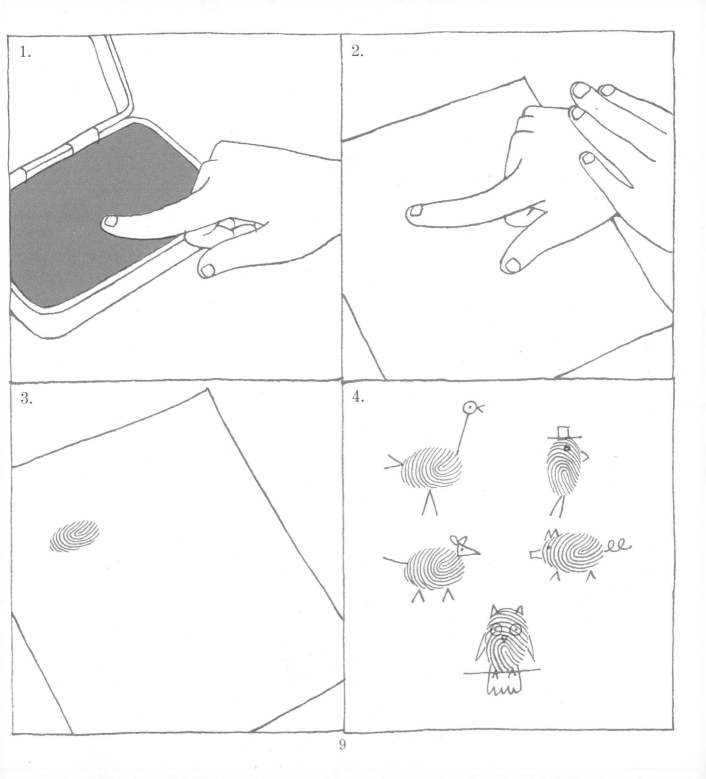

GLUE PRINTS

1. Take a piece of corrugated board or cardboard, and with a tube of Elmer's glue, draw a picture, squeezing lightly as you draw.

2. Let it dry for a few hours until the lines of the drawing are hard.

3. Pour some tempera paint or squeeze some water-base block-printing ink onto a cookie sheet or the back of a pie tin. Mix and smooth it with a palette knife. Then move a brayer back and forth in the color until it is well covered with the color.

4. Now apply the brayer to the raised glue drawing surface, moving it back and forth until all the lines of the drawing are well covered with color. Try not to let too much color touch the spaces between the lines. You may return the brayer to the cookie sheet to pick up more color as you need it.

   In printing from raised surfaces, some sort of absorbent paper is good. Rice paper is the best, but newsprint paper, available in pads, works well; and even some paper towels. It is also possible to use non-absorbent paper, but the effect will be somewhat different, as the ink or paint will remain more on the surface of the paper, and you will roll less ink or paint onto the printing surface.

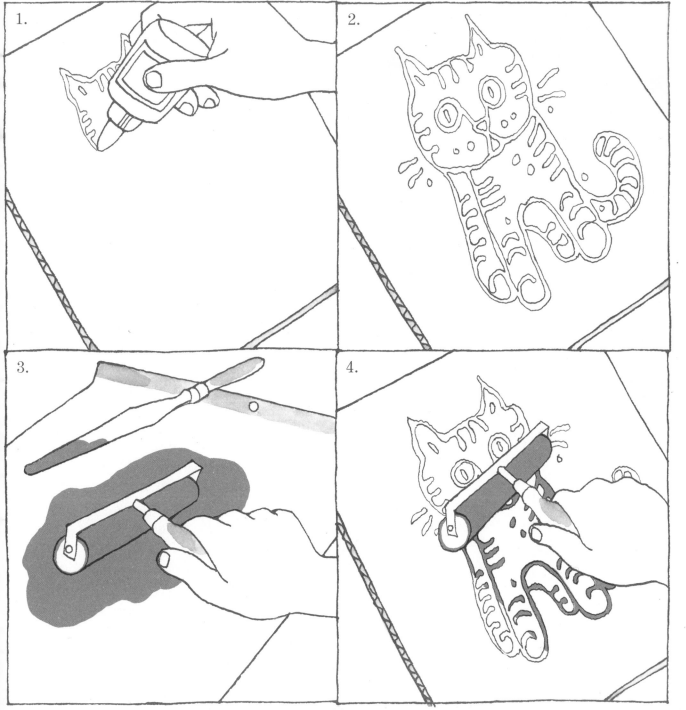

5. Hold the two top corners of a piece of paper down at the top edge of the cardboard surface with your fingers, while holding the opposite end of the paper lightly between the lips. Drop the paper from your lips before removing your fingers.

6. The paper is now resting on the inked glue drawing. Rub the back of the paper carefully but firmly all over with the bottom of the bowl of a soup spoon, trying not to press too hard in the low spaces between the lines.

7. Lift the paper a little at one corner to see if the color is coming off on the paper. If not, put the corner back down and rub some more. If the color *is* coming off on the paper, slowly lift off the whole sheet, starting as before at the corner.

8. There is your print. Notice that everything is backward, such as the tail on the opposite side. Now, to make the next print, roll paint or ink on the glue drawing again and repeat the process.

When you have as many prints as you need, clean up: Take a damp rag and rub lightly over the glue drawing surface to wipe off as much of the paint or ink as you can. Be careful not to let the cardboard get too wet. Then put it away to dry for future use. Wipe off the cookie sheet or pie tin with a damp rag, and clean the brayer on newspaper, rolling it back and forth while holding a damp rag against it.

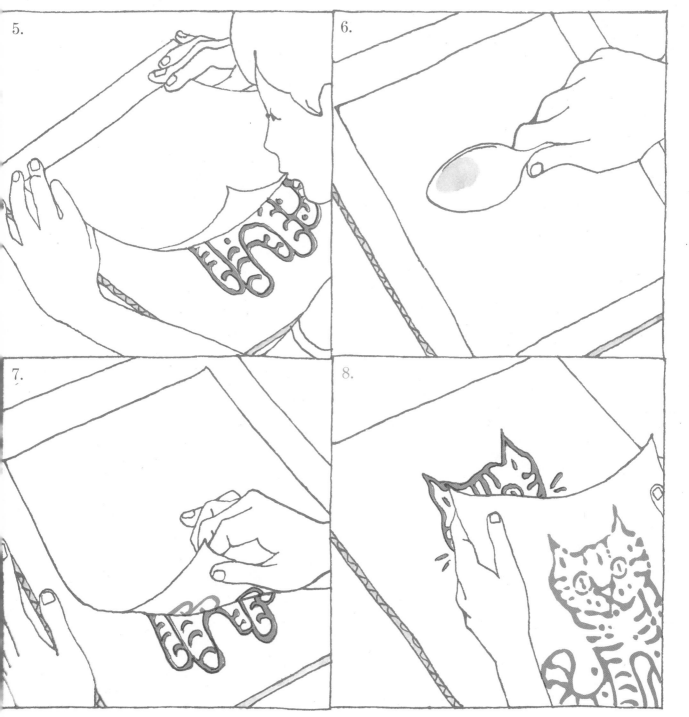

Glue print

Glue print

By Lizzy—age 11

15

COLLAGE PRINTS

1. Using the corrugated board or cardboard and Elmer's glue and assorted objects, glue objects to the board to form a picture or pattern. The example opposite uses buttons, string, burnt match, rice, and a paper clip, but there are thousands of possibilities. In many cases it is better to squeeze the glue onto the board first, and then place the objects onto the glue. Then allow the glue to harden.

2. Prepare the ink or tempera paint and roll onto the collage. You may have to move the brayer in many different directions and extra carefully over the bumps as the glued-down objects will be of different thicknesses.

3. Put a piece of paper down and rub with the spoon.

4. Peel off the paper after testing the corner.

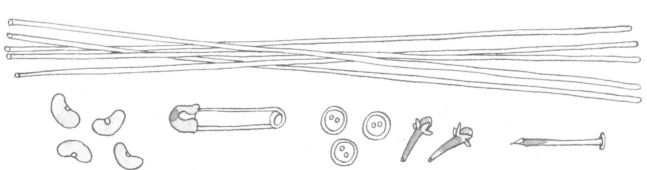

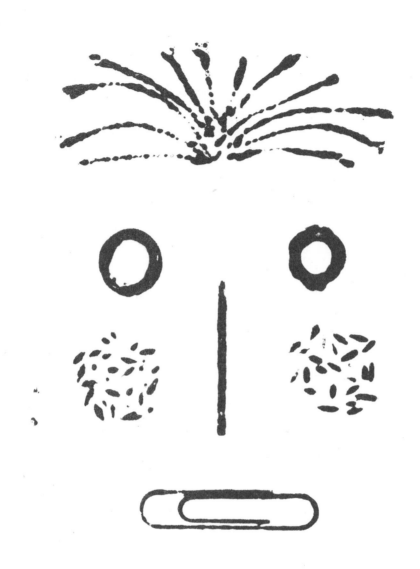

Collage print

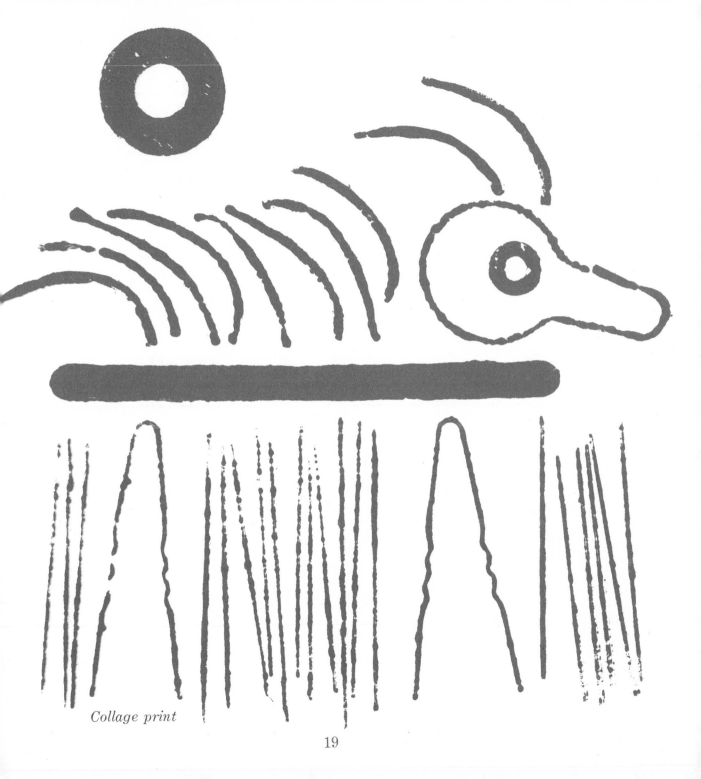

Collage print

19

POTATO PRINTS

1. Cut some potatoes in half with a fairly sharp knife, being very careful of fingers.

2. Cut a simple shape on the flat end of one of the halves.

3. Then cut shapes in the others. You now have a set of printing stamps to work with.

4. After stirring, pour some tempera paint into a small dish. Add a little water if it is too thick. It should be about the consistency of heavy cream.

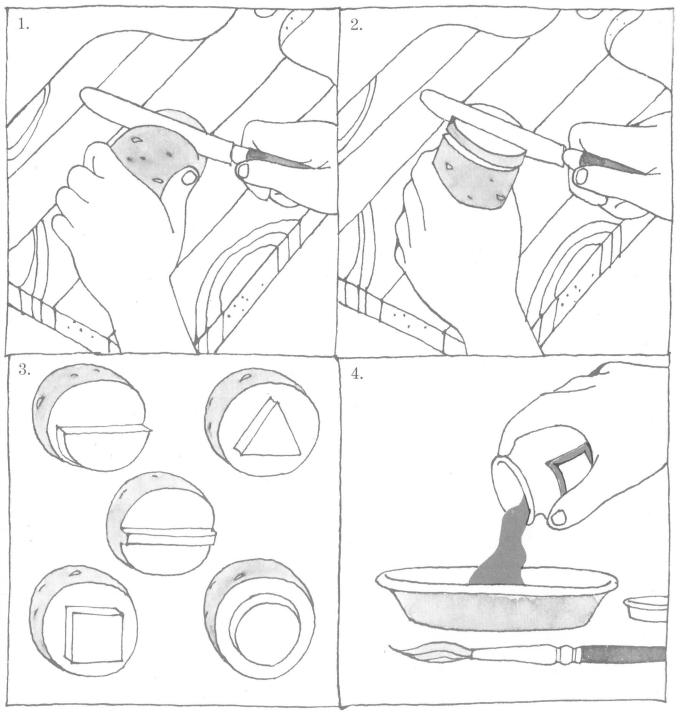

5. Dip a brush in the paint and apply it to the raised surface on the end of the potato half.

6. Then press it down firmly on a piece of white or colored paper.

7. Now do the same with another potato shape . . . and another.

8. There are many shapes you could cut, such as stars, plus signs, and so on.

Now try making pictures with different arrangements and all-over patterns. You can make your own gift-wrapping paper, or you can print on cloth. If possible, use two or more colors for variety.

In addition to potatoes, carrots and turnips can be used. They are harder to cut but work well for round shapes. Apples can also be used and are very easy to cut into printing shapes.

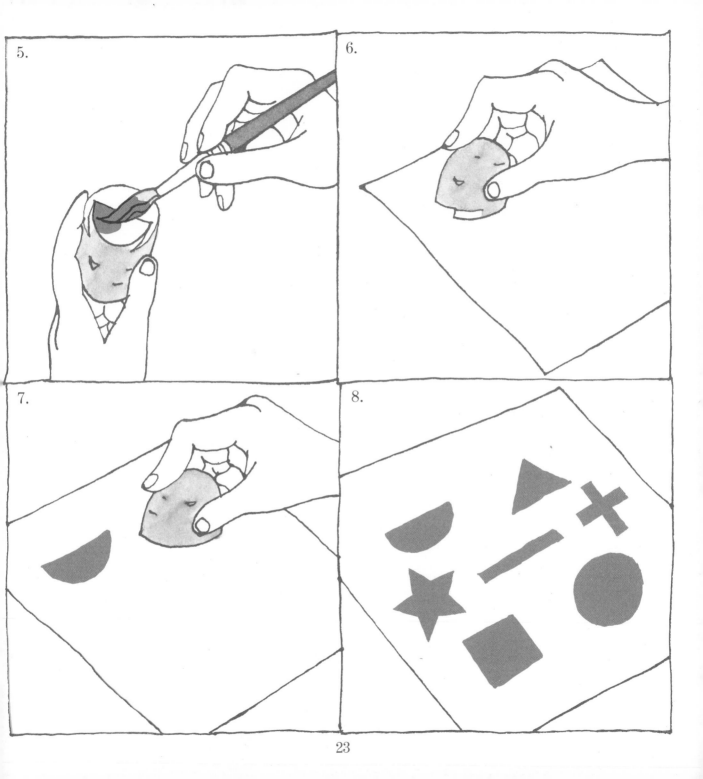

Potato print

By Olly—age 6

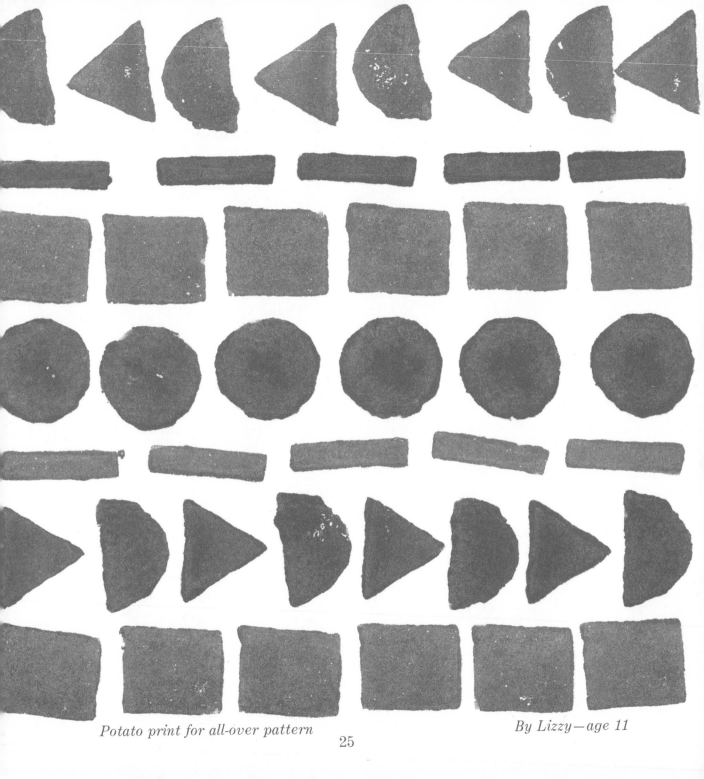

Potato print for all-over pattern

By Lizzy—age 11

SMOKE PRINTS

1. With a pair of pliers hold a key, a coin, a washer, a bent wire, a paper clip, or some other flat metal object over a candle flame until it is coated with black soot from the smoke.

2. Lay it down carefully on a piece of paper or thin balsa wood.

3. Press down on the object with a spoon or the end of the pliers.

4. Lift the object and there is the smoke print. You might add other objects to the print to form an interesting arrangement.

   Be very careful not to touch the metal objects with your fingers, as they will be hot.

Smoke print

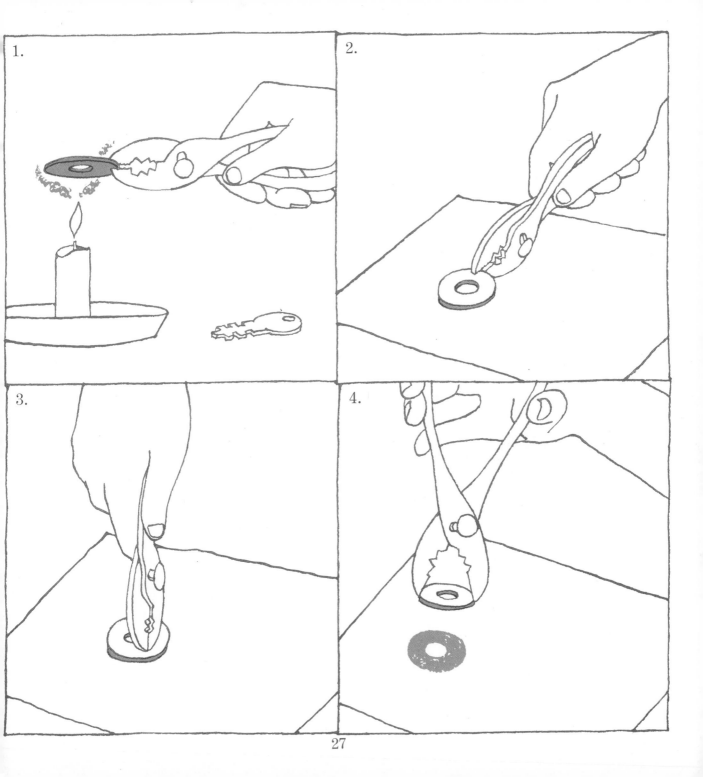

STYROFOAM PRINTS

1. A piece of Styrofoam such as is used for packing fragile objects can be gouged into with a large nail or screwdriver or even a hard stick to make a picture.

2. Pick up paint or ink on the brayer and roll onto the Styrofoam. You don't have to cover the entire surface.

3. Put a piece of paper down on the inked surface and rub with a spoon.

4. Lift off the paper after testing the corner. In your print the drawing will appear white against a colored background.

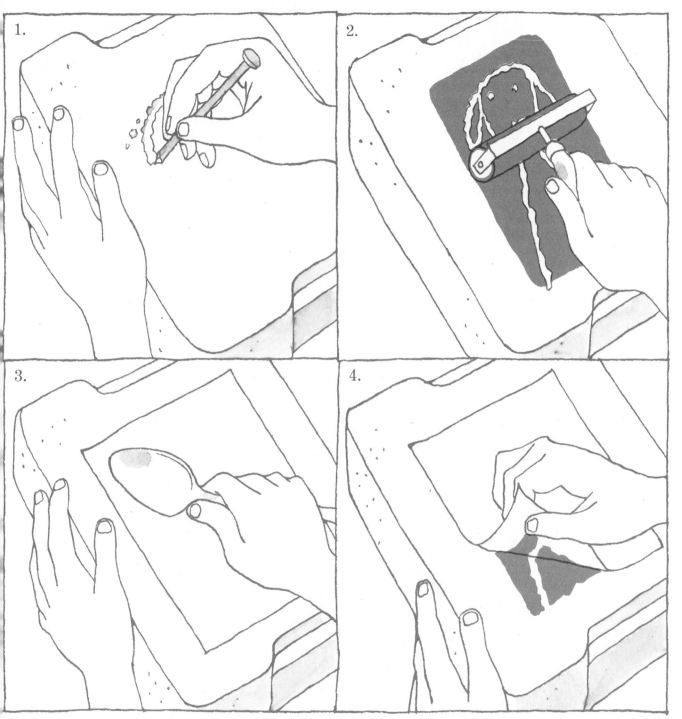

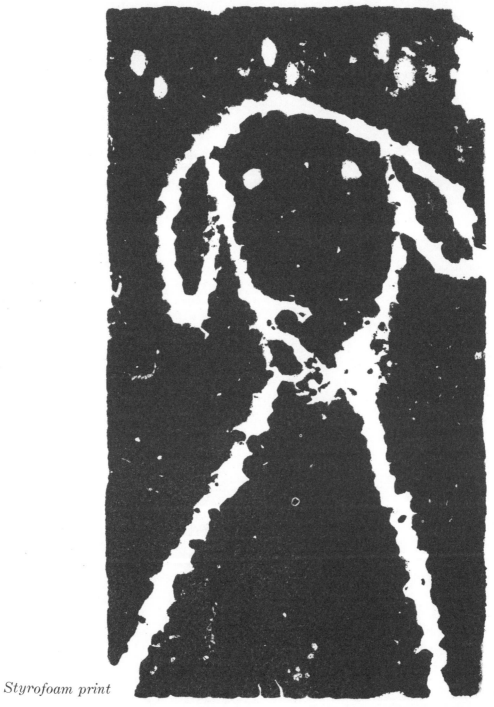

Styrofoam print   *By Olly—age 6*

Styrofoam print   *By Lizzy — age 11*

CARDBOARD CUT PRINTS

1. With an X-Acto knife cut shapes: circles, squares, strips, triangles, and others from corrugated board, cardboard, or poster board. You must have a wooden board or another heavy cardboard underneath to prevent cutting into your table. Some cardboard can be cut with scissors, however.

2. Assemble the shapes to form a picture or design and fasten them down onto another corrugated board or cardboard with Elmer's glue.

3. Apply ink to the raised surfaces with the brayer.

4. Put down your paper, rub with the spoon, lift off carefully after testing corner.

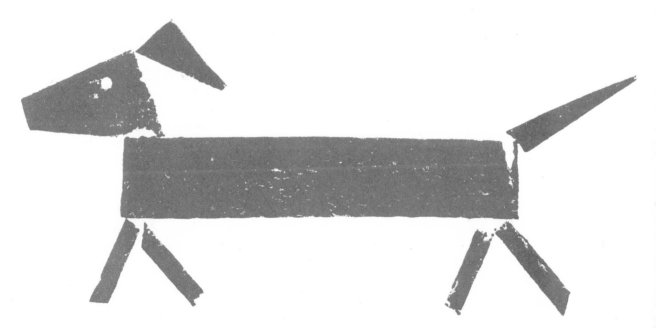

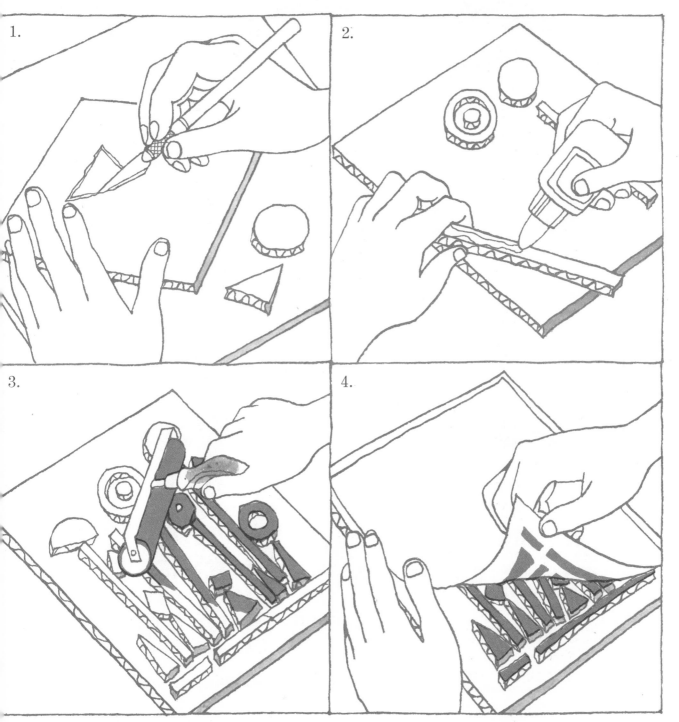

Cardboard cut print

Cardboard cut print

MONOTYPES

A monotype is a kind of print, because it is an impression taken from another surface. It is different, however, because only one print can be taken, although the one piece of paper can be put down on the painted and repainted surface many times to build up a more interesting pattern or design. You might like to have several jars of tempera paint of different colors for this.

1. On a cookie sheet or the back of a shallow enamelware baking pan, paint a picture, putting the paint on fairly thick and wet so that it will not dry too quickly. Make the painting smaller than the paper you intend to use.

2. Put the piece of paper down carefully onto the wet painted surface, holding the corners as explained before. Paint small cross marks on the cookie sheet at the two top corners of the paper as a guide to positioning when you put the paper back down again.

3. Rub all over gently with your hand, a rolling pin or the clean brayer.

4. Lift off the paper after testing at one corner.

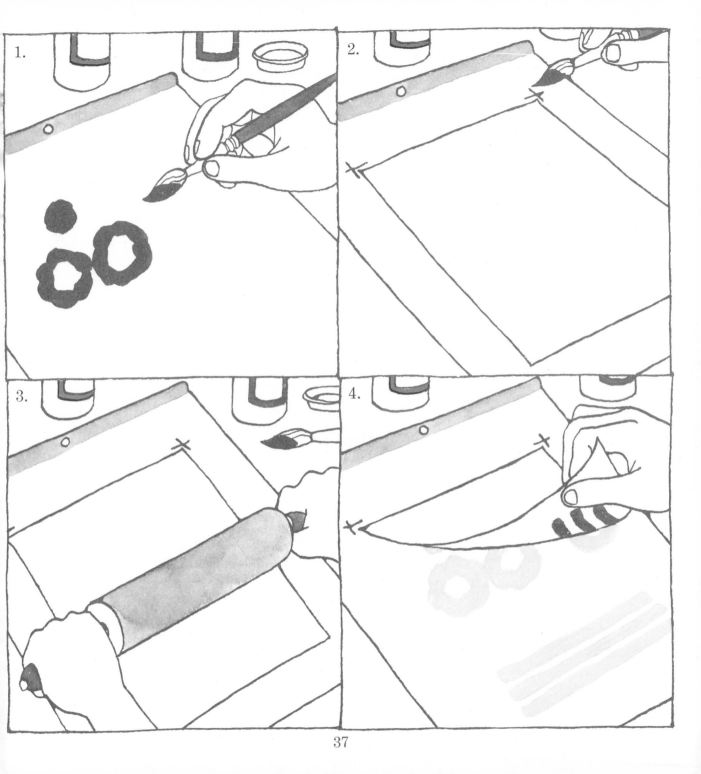

5. After the paint is dry on the paper, paint some more on the cookie sheet here and there in other colors, to add to the print.

6. Then put the paper back down again, lining up the two top corners of the paper with the cross marks left on the cookie sheet. Then roll with the rolling pin and peel off. Put the paper back down as many times as you feel are needed to add more interest to your print, of course cleaning off the cookie sheet and painting a little more each time.

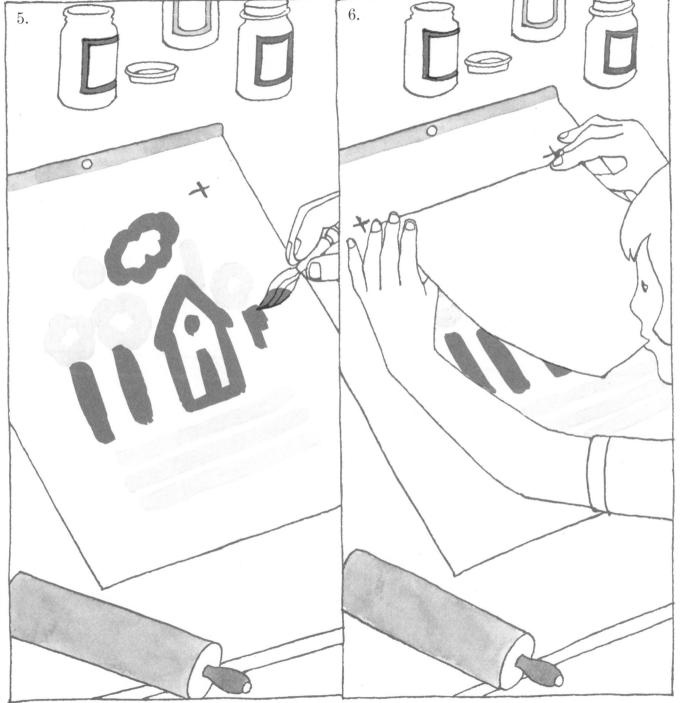

Monotype

41

LINOLEUM CUT PRINTS

Pieces of linoleum, a linoleum cutting tool or gouge, and tubes of water-base block-printing ink can be bought at art supply stores and some stationery stores. Some linoleum is mounted on blocks of wood but for our purpose the unmounted kind is better.

1. You can plan your linoleum cut by drawing directly on the surface of the linoleum lightly with crayon or soft pencil or with a brush and thin paint. Or you can plan it on lightweight paper or tracing paper and then trace it onto the linoleum with carbon paper.

2. For the easiest cut you can simply cut lines into the surface of the linoleum with the gouge which, when printed, will give you white lines against a colored background. As you cut you hold and push the gouge with your right hand (if you're right-handed), at the same time steadying it with your left, to prevent the tool from slipping and cutting too far. The heel of the left hand rests on the linoleum to help hold it in place. If you wish to have colored lines and areas against a white background you must cut away at the sides of and between these lines and areas.

3. Roll ink onto the linoleum cut.

4. Put down a piece of paper, rub with your spoon, lift carefully.

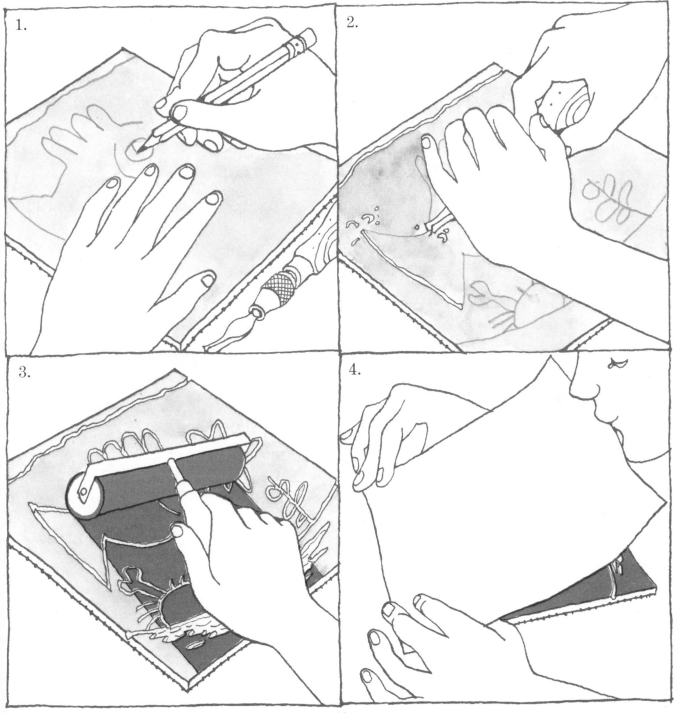

Linoleum cut print   *By Olly—age 6*

44

Linoleum cut print   *By Lizzy—age 11*

TWO-COLOR PRINTS

Linoleum cuts work very well for two-color prints. You will need two pieces of linoleum the same size, two tubes of water-base block-printing ink of two different colors, one tube of white ink if you wish to lighten a color, two colored pencils, and a piece of carbon paper.

1. Plan a two-color drawing smaller than the linoleum, on light-weight paper or tracing paper cut to the size of the linoleum. Draw two small triangles near the top of the paper away from the drawing. You must remember which part of the drawing is to be the first color and which is to be the second. It is possible to use colored pencils to show this.

2. With carbon paper under the drawing, and with the paper taped to the first piece of linoleum at the top, trace down the drawing for the first of the colors, including the two small triangles.

3. Then take up the paper with the drawing and tape it to the other piece of linoleum. Now, with the carbon paper underneath, trace the part of the drawing for the second color, plus the small triangles again, down onto this second piece of linoleum.

4. Dig away (about 1/8 inch deep) at both pieces of linoleum with the gouge, cutting in and around your design until ready for printing. Cut around the small triangles so that they can be inked.

5. Take a tube of ink of the color you wish to print first and squeeze some of it onto part of a cookie sheet. You can lighten the value of the color with a little white ink if you like. Mix and smooth it with a palette knife.

6. Move the brayer back and forth in the ink until it is evenly covered. Then onto the linoleum cut, remembering to ink the two small triangles at the top.

7. Now, alternately inking, putting the paper down, lifting, inking, putting paper down again, print as many in this color as you wish, perhaps five for a start. When you are more advanced at printmaking, you can print many more of an edition, as it is called.

8. You now have five prints but they are only in the one color. Clean off the linoleum cut with a damp rag and put it aside for possible printing in the future. Start inking linoleum cut number two, including the two small triangles, with the second color, which you will have squeezed onto another part of the cookie sheet. Your five prints taken from linoleum cut number one should now go down on linoleum cut number two, one at a time, with rolling and inking, rubbing and lifting, in between. Each time you put down a print onto the second color you must line up the small triangles on the print with those on linoleum cut number two. With an absorbent paper the ink usually shows through to the back of the paper,

The small triangles are only for the purpose of aligning the two colors.

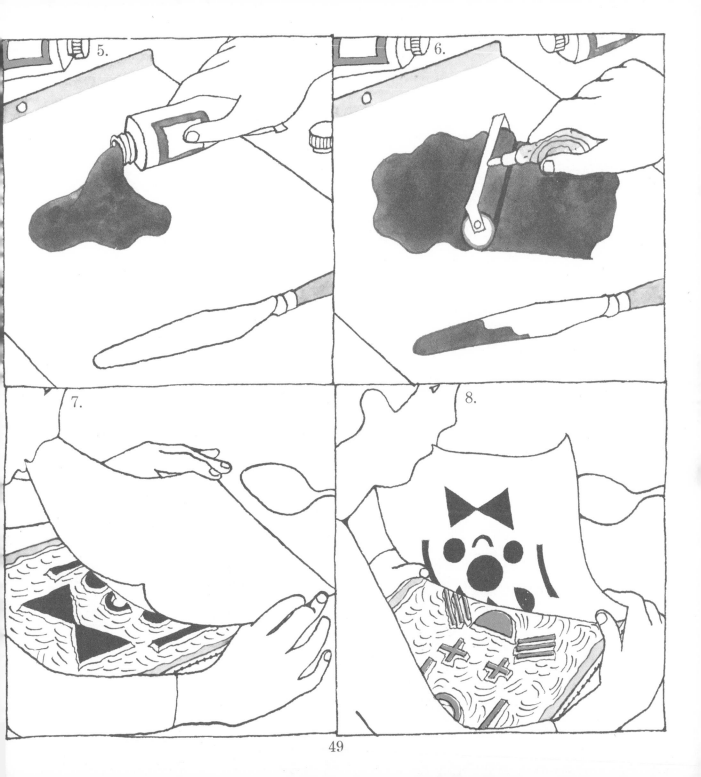

50

2-color linoleum cut print

51

WOODCUT PRINTS

To make a woodcut you will need a piece of fairly soft wood at least 3/8 inch thick and large enough to rest both hands on. Also needed is a rounded gouge for wood about 3/16 inch wide at the end, or even better, two gouges, one 1/8 inch wide and one 1/4 inch wide, an X-Acto knife, carbon paper, and tracing paper.

1. You can apply a drawing or design directly onto the wood with a brush and ink or thin tempera paint.

2. Or you can plan it on thin paper or tracing paper and then trace it down onto the wood with a harder pencil or pointed stick, using carbon paper between your drawing and the wood; or by blackening the back of the drawing with a soft pencil and tracing through without carbon paper.

3. It is possible to cut a design directly into the wood with a gouge, holding and pushing with the right hand while steadying the gouge with the left. When printed you will have white lines showing against a colored background.

4. It is more difficult to cut away *around* lines and areas. For this start with the X-Acto knife. Cut into the wood about 1/16 inch deep along the edges of lines and areas. Then turn the board around and cut along close to the other cuts, 1/16 or 1/8 inch away, forming a V-shaped trench along the sides of the raised parts. Hold the board still with your left hand while you work, but keep your hand out of the path of the knife.

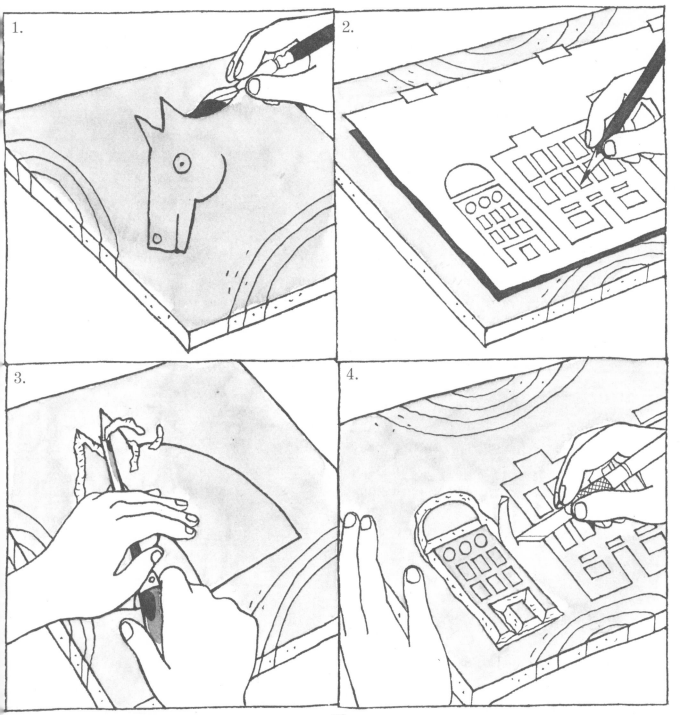

5. Now take the gouge and, holding it as before, scoop out wood around and in between the lines and areas. Scoop out to a depth of at least 1/8 inch, coming up to the trenches or grooves you have already cut with the knife. Be careful not to slip and cut into a raised line. If you have two gouges, use the narrower one for small spaces. When scooping out, work along with the direction of the wood grain where possible.

6. Rub the woodcut lightly with a dry rag to remove any wood shavings or crumbs of wood. Then squeeze ink onto a cookie sheet or pie tin and smooth it with a palette knife. Apply the brayer to the ink, rolling back and forth until it is evenly covered. Then onto the woodcut, being careful to cover all parts evenly, not too thick and not too thin. You will know this after one or two test prints. You can thin the ink slightly with a drop or two of water, but blend it well together with the palette knife.

7. Put down the paper, holding the two top corners with your fingers and the lower edge lightly between the lips. Then drop the lower edge. Rub all over carefully but firmly with the bottom of the bowl of the soup spoon. Then lift after testing one corner to see if it is printing well enough.

8. It is possible to make woodcut prints of more than one color. For this you can refer to the section on two-color linoleum prints, substituting wood for linoleum.

Woodcut print

2-color woodcut print

Harlow Rockwell was born in Buffalo, New York. He attended Pratt Institute, The Art Students League, L'Academie Julien in Paris, Blackburn's Lithograph Workshop, and studied with Adja Junkers at the New School. His prints have been exhibited at the Library of Congress in Washington. He has worked as an advertising art director and designer and has won the Art Directors Club Gold Medal for three years in a row.

Mr. Rockwell has collaborated with his wife, Anne, on several children's books including *Olly's Polliwogs*, *Toad*, and *Head to Toe*, but this is the first book he has both written and illustrated by himself.

The Rockwells live in Old Greenwich, Connecticut, with their three children, Hannah, Elizabeth, and Oliver.

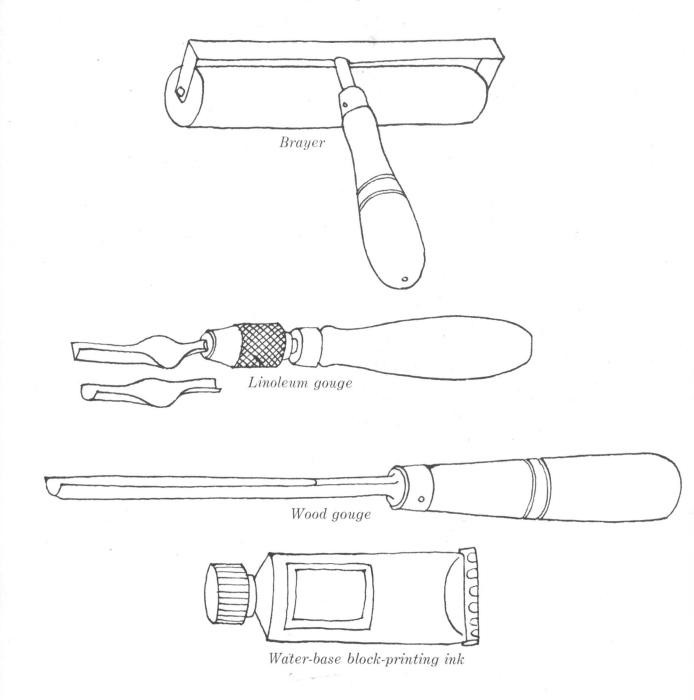

Brayer

Linoleum gouge

Wood gouge

Water-base block-printing ink